From Melancholic To Diminished

MELISSA ANN MEADE

ISBN: 978-1-79066010-0

Any references to events, real people, or real places have been marked in quotations, changed, or are have been altered. Protecting a person's privacy and image is something I pride myself on.

Front cover images designed by Canva.com and property of Canva.com

First printing edition 2019

Melissa Ann Meade

www.melissaannmeade.com

*THIS BOOK IS DEDICATED TO
"THE CAPRICORNS."*

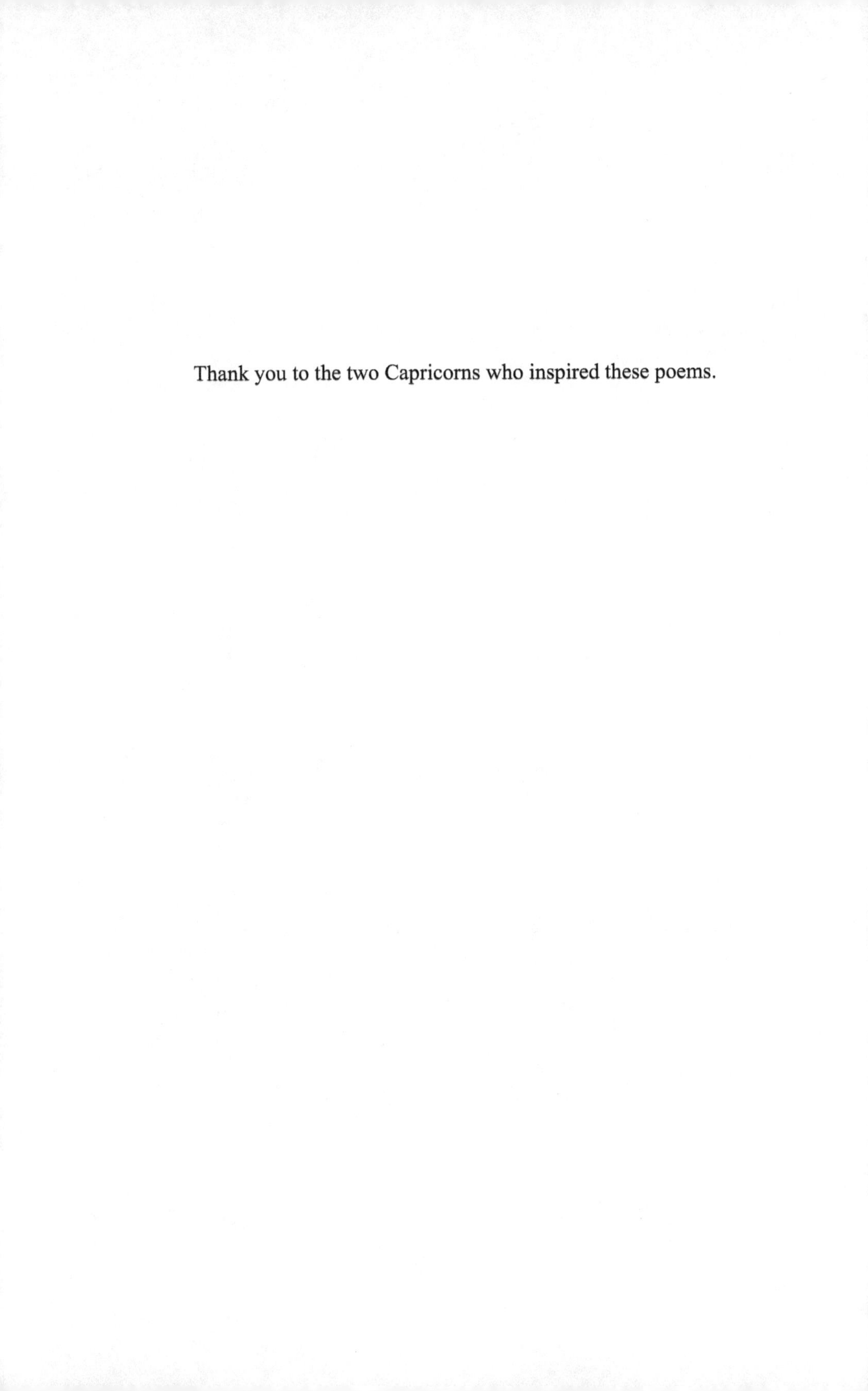

Thank you to the two Capricorns who inspired these poems.

From Melancholic to Diminished

Introduction

Diminished, this title finally dawned on me one night as an ex-boyfriend texted me after months of not speaking. The last time we had spoken, I had told him to contact me when he was single. He contacted me but *was not single* after all that time.

I originally had the words *Mistress* or *Second* as the title, but I was and am more than that. I had diminished myself and I had let all of them *diminish* me over the course of the past few years of my life. Now I value myself and they do not deserve me. I owe them though because you are about to read some intense poetry. Without them, I would not have been inspired. I look at it with gratitude because I am thankful that they provoked me to write some pretty potent poems.

Two men have inspired these poems. The worst of them being solely *emotional*. One was *physical* and *emotional*. I always had hoped I would be **chosen**. Why were they drawn to me? Why do they remain drawn to me? What is it about me that makes me so magnetic to *taken* men? Seriously, I would love to know.

Are they dark souls too? Do they see the darkness in my eyes that draw them in? Is it because I am "*the anti-girlfriend*" because I am independent? I am too independent. I chose them for the challenge and because it was always easier to detach and walk away.

I was always granted false hopes and false promises. I fell for their shit and they fell for mine. There will be no more of that. I value and respect myself too much. What we both did was not fair not just to us, but to others.

I truly feel empathy for them because they do not live a life of freedom and will probably never get that beautiful experience. They cower in comfort. I feel fierce in my freedom and now know they did not and do not deserve me because it is not fair to me.

This is a series of poems from relationships in which I was **diminished**. *Melancholic-the central theme to my life and a cyclic pattern of poor decisions with powerless males. I am thankful for being* **diminished** *and feeling* **melancholic**. *I produced some epic content for my readers.*

EXISTENCE

I exist and am a sudden thought
When you are drunk and alone
When you're sober, I then am not
Your heart hardens back to stone

Something so simple, you make complex
The mental mazes you make, complicate
You put up walls and then begin to perplex
Yet, somehow, you still manage to fascinate

I have feelings and that's all
You make it a grand equation
Something simple and small
I had not a single expectation

TEMPTATION

You brought up temptation
You stated that it was there
Directing me to devastation
As your feet went nowhere

Repeated words "I cannot cheat"
The only words you could speak
The only words you could repeat
Did I somehow make you weak?

Feeling twinges of rejection
Reveling with rue and regret
Not one act of any affection
Physical needs were unmet

Let you into something so deep
I made a big and blatant blunder
A promise to myself I didn't keep
Now I'm broken and torn asunder

11/4/17

PARTY OF THREE

You can have a girl at home
And also a girl on the side
You can continue to roam
But, eventually, you decide

To just have your cake
To have it and eat it too
One of them you will break
Oh, the damage you will do

There is no fair competition
As one remains in the dark
Constant words of repetition
As you leave each with a mark

A dangerous game you play
With fire, you always burn
Perhaps, we all walk away
Too scared to choose a turn

Two hearts then become three
Hearts shattering, then broken
You were too blind to even see
The weapons you had spoken

I have stepped back, free of this
A situation I had to surely leave
You were my heart, I will miss
Promises that I wanted to believe

RESPECT

Filled me with craze
And some delusion
Your mental maze
An obvious illusion

You wouldn't come near
Wouldn't even touch me
You couldn't even hear
You couldn't really see

So now I disappear
From your limited life
A rejection so clear
You "*respect*" your wife

11/4/17

ZOMBIE

Pompously boasting that I was too attached
Such magical mazes your mind had hatched

Churned spite when called *cold and callous*
Claiming compassion, comprised of malice

A zombie with emptiness and no affection
Sniffing out flesh in every single direction

The first organ you go for is a beating heart
No matter what, it's where you always start

Blackened eyes and completely dead inside
Feasting on whomever is even by your side

Clots of blood seeping down your bony chin
Satiated, your face displays a shit-eating grin

Feasting on the carnage until there is no more
Giving apocalyptic gifts-destruction and gore

LAST WORD

I am a little banged up and a bit broken
Words you written, words you'd spoken

There is truth in the saying history repeats
Suffering the same blows and same defeats

Same verbiage typed by different fingers
Words that haunt as hopelessness lingers

The newest assortment, "complain and whine"
By another one blindly believing he is divine

I am smart, but lacking common sense
Words make my illness more immense

Proudly boasting how I had been discarded
This destitute once again been disregarded

Words are bombs that they blast
Love is my dream fading too fast

A writer, I always had to have the last word
Yet, slinging words makes me sound absurd

This time my plan is to sink them with silence
Words worse than a weapon causing violence

Words to a writer the harshest weapon by choice
Fueling me with self-doubt and stealing my voice

11/14/18

FACELESS

The words I write, they cannot face
They then stop, giving up the chase

The truth hurts and obviously so do I
I once was the only star in your sky

You told me that I was the brightest
You proved to me I was the whitest

Now you demoralize and demean
Acting if I was nothing ever seen

Ask to see my content so I show
Feeling confident that we'd grow

Once they read, they stop all the caring
Bombarding me with words so blaring

I question why I then get discarded
I always leave my gates unguarded

Can they not face who they are?
A slice, pain, and an eternal scar

Do they run because they see what they did?
Contributing to this pathetic life I want to rid

11/14/18

EA-11/14/17

This was a full-blown emotional affair
That had only one direction, no where

I saw how you tugged and felt your wedding band
Each time we saw each other (always your demand)

Constant comparisons of me to your wife
It seemed that a piece of you envied my life

It must be stifling wearing your "moral values mask"
In all that moral bullshit you stay and fucking bask

You kept telling me that you couldn't cheat
Since it wasn't physical, that's your retreat

You emphasized family commitment
Yet, your actions were quite different

I shouldn't have answered the phone
Knowing, I would feel suddenly alone

You told me to not sell myself short
That mind of yours loves to distort

You fear judgment if you separate
You cannot accept this as a fate

Yet, repeatedly spew the word "divorce"
We both know, it won't happen, of course

I am finished being compared to her
All you exhibit is how you're insecure

You said we were kindred spirits at lunch
That was some bullshit, in fact a bunch

You pulled off the most epic rejection
Validating me-one giant imperfection

THREE YEARS

It has been three years
We still keep in touch
Our passion still appears
Can I love you that much?

We still kiss the same as the first night
Fueled with depth, intensity, and fire
As our lips meet, our souls re-ignite
I ache, yearn, and swell with desire

Why can't both of us ever move on?
Why can't we even attempt to resist?
Time slips into the past and is gone
Yet, our passion continues to persist

You're always there for me in times of need
Even though I asked you to just leave me be
A fire you still fuel, a hunger you still feed
My heart suffers burns that are third degree

Perhaps, one day, I will be strong enough to leave
Finally, after all these years, maybe I'll break free
One day, we will be together, I want to still believe
Yet, that decision is up to you and it is not up to me

4/18/18

EX FILES #1 4/7/18

Last night, I thought about leaving a trace behind
As I laid up all night, hoping she would catch us
Finally seeing after years, our bodies intertwined
Witnessing our love and how we act so treasonous

I hoped maybe she would detect my perfumed scent
Or discover a single, long strand of dyed, blonde hair
Smelling a familiar fragrance you picked up with no intent
That you wore when you came home each time from "*there*"

I fantasize about her discovering us and sending you away
Sending you nowhere to go, except to me, at my front door
I would openly welcome you in and offer you a place to stay
You would be with me forever, but why choose your whore?

It felt so incredible, you wanted to stay inside and I agreed
I also promised you that I would take the morning after pill
I still have two days left to take it, but I have yet to precede
Maybe, I want free will or want you to pay half of the bill

I feel somewhat hopeful because we may have conceived
I would finally have the perfect man and father to my child
Yet, I have to take Plan B so we both are calm and relieved
I know, us as parents together, a thought too crazy and wild

We parted ways three years ago, but have never moved on
Such passion, intensity, and love that we can never ignore
Remaining with her, yet I haven't seen you good and gone
I want you back, pick up where we left off, and even more

We were supposed to end up together and planned to marry
Yet, I did not choose you and I mistakenly chose my career
My undying love and the burden of you I still have to carry
I live everyday with my mistake, and all I want is you here

EX FILES #2 4/7/18

A night full of poppers and wine
In bed, we were one; connected
Felt incredible and I felt so fine
My body, you totally respected

You didn't want me to be alone
You made love to me all night
Candle burning, romantic tone
You promised me I'd be alright

We passionately and deeply kissed
Every touch, I found to stimulate
How I've longed, how I've missed
As I begged for you to penetrate

I got to gaze deeply into your eyes
Sensing everything you had to give
Why haven't I wanted to recognize
That you are air wanting me to live

I asked you to be wild, nasty, and rough
Yet, you only could be sweet and gentle
I come to realize that love was enough
As you were so kind and complemental

I didn't want the night to end, I felt alive
Intense and I deemed it "*the best night*"
So selfless that you did not once deprive
My eyes once dark, suddenly went bright

You made love to me, gave me all you had
Compliments and kisses giving me meaning
I soon exited the darkness, no longer felt sad
I am beyond grateful for your act of intervening

ONE AND THE OTHER

One states to me that my life has no meaning
The other says I make him want to be better
One's cruelty-spewed words are demeaning
Each inspire poetry and each given a letter

One claims I'm hyperbolic and complain
The other says I inspire and have reason
Both, happen to inflict poetry and pain
I am the other woman, the toxic treason

One has never even given me one kiss
The other gives me every, single inch
Fucked up that the both of them I miss
My heart, they both seemed to lynch

One keeps me mentally calm and gives peace
The other rattles my cage and primal hunger
One has never provided any sexual release
The other fucks me as if I am much younger

They have both fucked with my head
They have both fucked with my heart
Hopefulness, I have not a single shred
As they choose to not be near, but apart

Perhaps, I will meet a man with no strings
And someone with no puppeteer to please
Someone with no baggage, one with wings
And I will finally be granted a life of ease

4/8/18

SECRETS

Your secrets are safe with me
As I hope mine are with you
Sanity is what you will see
As we forget and start anew

I am going to disappear
Vanish from your life
Leave you free and clear
To still respect your wife

11/4/17

WHISPERER

Your wife's mind would be going into overdrive
If she knew "*another woman*" was attentive to you
Yet, you kept planting seeds in my mind to thrive
Told me you needed me to see you make it through

Honestly, would she even really care?
I bet my name you didn't even mention
As you remained ignorant and unaware
Seeking and accepting all the attention

I followed, respected, and abided by **your** rules
Putting up with your pathetic codependency
Her and I are both naïve and fucked-up fools
Drawn to your hollow disillusioned tendency

I fell hard for you, you selfish fuck
Fabrications in my mangled mind
In a stagnant life, you'll be stuck
Remaining harsh, *cold*, and unkind

Do you think you're the first married man?
So many unhappy men, I know the ropes
Sneaking up on me as I was part of a plan
Laying amongst dashed dreams and hopes

Do you or did really ever love her?
Does she even love or attend to you?
I am always the husband **whisperer**
Surviving the hell you put me through

While she needs your attention
I never once placed any pressure
You misconstrued my intention
Making my wounds even fresher

Being "*another woman*" I accept as my calling
I told you to live your life and was fine with all
You never once stopped me when I was falling
When I confessed, you knew you broke my wall

Or the boyfriend whisperer if they aren't married
Never good enough for anything beyond that
Always sought-after during times of trouble
I need to live all alone protected in a bubble

11/4/17

SHE AND I

She will never go away, she will always be there
You will stay because she tugs at your heart strings
I unfortunately do not have an eternity to wait here
I do have other places, other people, other things

She is attached and is sucking the life out of you
Wearing away your soul, you are fucking trapped
Preferring old comforts, terrified of anything new
I see your disability and that you are handicapped

She engulfs you whole and I somehow get forgotten
I am a disposable detachment you set and sought out
Unhappiness sometimes can make you so damn rotten
And then decorate me in self-destruction and self-doubt

I am not one to live in someone's dark shadow
I personally do not deserve such oppression
I am not a mind or object you can just borrow
Or an outlet for you to voice every transgression

I want you to be happy and I want you to smile;
To realize your own magnitude and full potential
To realize that you don't have to hide your beguile
And live your life with files stamped "confidential"

October 2017

INNOCENCE

You act like you were an innocent party
An unwilling participant in this game
To think I preyed on you forcefully
Shows me the depths of your delusions
I was the only person in your corner
Your only cheerleader, your only fan
You sadly mistook this for love
No, it was my mistake to be weak
I should have not allowed myself to feel
I should have not opened up my mind
I should have covered my eyes and ears
I should have ignored you and walked away

11/4/17

FORBIDDEN

I always lent you an ear
Listening to your struggle
Comparisons to her I'd hear
My mind began to juggle

I tried to give you tips
I felt such discomfort
Lies spilt from your lips
Emotions you'd extort

As you tugged on your ring
Dishing every dirty detail
Non-verbally I was a thing
You'd toss along the trail

Discussing your **dead marriage**
Initially began in a friendly manner
Something you could not disparage
Your **vows** meant more than her

I began to develop feelings
Something I could not control
Pulled me into dirty dealings
A **mindfuck** swallowing me whole

I set all of my reasoning aside
Knowing I would be rejected
Deciding to take a regretted ride
Never nurtured, only neglected

I laid it all on the line
Lost you as a friend
Saw you lack a spine
Now I write "**the end**"

11/3/17

MARRED

Constant complaints of corrosion
Of your **_maimed matrimony_**
I suffered an emotional explosion
Listening to your tragic testimony

Unhappiness is all you uttered
Dishing depression and doubts
Just like bread, I was buttered
Perplexed by pointless pouts

You built bullshit _boundaries_
Forced me into a forgotten fool
I was just one of your foundries
Utilized me as if I was just a tool

Subduing me into stupidity
I'm destined for destruction
Voiced I had zero validity
Words equating my reduction

Perpetual, pathetic patterns
Drowning in disappointment
Covered in scars and burns
You left me with no ointment

Jaded in judgment, reaped in rejection
Fashionably flawed and feeble to a fault
An expected error and definite dejection
Accepted abandonment after your assault

Staging strength when I am really weak
Inconsistent intimacy causing honest harm
Your critical carelessness made me meek
Boundless blunders from cynicism and charm

11/3/17

SWAT

You went onto surveil and barge into my life
Forcefully kicking the dead-bolted door in
Constantly mentioning *dead marriage* and *wife*
And a new adventure you were about to begin

Prodding my mind you continued to flirt
With me and all of my deranged *danger*
You brought back the pain and all the hurt
As you became less and less of a stranger

I wish you would've kept your distance
Setting imposed *boundaries* right away
I would've maintained better resistance
And would have chosen to run not stay

Now my mind is flooded with thoughts
Of how you act so *cold* and misconstrue
I keep trying to disconnect damaged dots
To reach you and actually make it through

I wish to one day forget
To be strong to move on
However, I feel no regret
I'm past your phenomenon

LIFELESS

One minute, you're headed for divorce
And the house is going on the market
Phrases you would go on and reinforce
As you began the overwhelming onset

Then suddenly, you are committed
Saying you can't fuck up your family
Once a presence, then left omitted
Formerly collective, now a calamity

Truth is, your marriage is already fucked
Two steps forward then three steps back
Dreams dried and ***diminished*** as you sucked
All my emotions with your verbal attack

Go on and keep living a limited, lifeless life
Oh the heavy dead weight you have to carry
As you stay stagnant by respecting your wife
Acting as if you were held by force to marry

11/4/17

REASON

I hope you ended up washing the sheets
And also, the comforter and pillow cases
Our history, constantly cycles and repeats
Each time together, I know my heart races

I hope I didn't leave any strands of hair behind
I hope I didn't leave a trace of my perfumed scent
Those sheets all bundled, soiled, and intertwined
Started to kiss, then, well we know where it went

I made certain to pick up every piece of lingerie
As, I prepared to do my walk and drive of shame
I wanted to lay with you and wanted to truly stay
I questioned if your intentions were true or a game

Sometimes, I feel sorry for the live-in-girlfriend
Who leaves you unhappy and sexually deprived
Yet, you trudge on- the relationship needs to end
I think I am the reason you stayed and survived

You say you can't end it; she has nowhere to live
Yet, you sleep on the couch and she gets the bed
That bed where I got all the love you had to give
Why stay in a relationship that's stagnant and dead

Somehow, I find myself waiting up in the stands
Cheering you on, as if I am your one and only fan
Yet, I choose to live instead of sitting on my hands
Pondering if you're sincere or if you are a con-man

I think you maybe want her to learn of your deception
Years and years, we each continue, to commit treason
So deep, never even using any form of contraception
Yet, why do you stay there, I will soon need a reason

HYPOCRITE

You live a humdrum life
Pretending you are perfect
Bitching about your strife
Mentioning my flaws to deflect

Your mirror is too shattered to self-reflect
Complaining about things you can change
You possess zero concern and self-respect
Drudging along as you destroy and derange

You chose and continue to your life's design
Yet, you preach to me I'm in charge of mine
Chastising me to get up, take stage and shine
Cowering in the crowd, mistaken you're divine

Why am I viewed in such a poor way?
What is so fucking perfect about you?
What made you decide on me to prey?
Left me for dead when you withdrew

Now, I have to heal my damage and pain
From your selfish and evil mind game
You messed me up by fucking my brain
Yet, somehow, I am the one you blame

11/4/17

ONE

All I need and want is one that can commit full-time
I do not need two part-timers with limited availability
Maybe I do want a love in my life, a partner in crime
I'm done always being a secret and now want visibility

It is not fair that you get me part time and her full time
I struggle with your language because I want to believe
She has the value of a dollar bill and I'm valued as a dime
I have a glimmer of hope that your dreams you'll achieve

I had one part-time and kept refusing to take on a second
Then our shit fell apart, and I opted for a similar position
Then I rushed into his arms when he again had beckoned
I was fragile, frail, and weak in a very unstable condition

He with no hesitation came to comfort me and we had sex
When it was over, I was crying hysterically thinking of you
Thinking he did something wrong; my comforting, loving ex
I felt so awful that I hurt him when he wanted to start anew

A few days later, he invited me over to his house, I went
He told me that he would not let me spend the night alone
Candles burning, he expressed how I caused him discontent
Each time I refused him due to dabbling with the unknown

He told me he was there for months and was waiting for me
He wants to give it another try since I am now back in town
Three years have gone and his love back then, I still can see
The passion between the two of us has not yet cooled down

I love him, am in love with you, and I have to logically think
You make me feel alive and he does too where we are restricted
Maybe you'll both be gone when I open up my eyes after I blink
The two types of love I'm feeling are so wrong and contradicted

4/11/18

IDEAL IDIOT

I fall for every fake fuck
They accept the attention
Like vampires, they suck
My dry soul loses retention

Blaming me for it all
My kindness is a flaw
Break down my wall
Grab my mind and maul

Giving too much of myself
Being too fucking generous
Cohabitation on an ice shelf
Ran me over with your bus

Am I am ideal idiot or a hopeless romantic?
I hate to admit but I am so fucking hopeless
Continued to put up with every asshole antic
Jamming it in and making me a manic mess

Mistaking your mind-fuck for love
I should have been more self-aware
What do you have to be proud of?
Staying still and going nowhere?

FOUR LINERS

PHONE CALL

I wouldn't have answered the phone
If I knew you'd chill me to the bone
You wanted us to be on the same page
That is to only perform on your stage

11/3/17

TRIBUTE

I got your message loud and clear
I will quickly backpedal out of here
You will never again get shit from me
Except these tributes from my tragedy

11/3/17

OVERCAST

On the beach
There is no sun
You're out of reach
Because you're done

February 2018

THREE

It has been over three years
And we still keep in touch
Passion never disappears
Can I love you that much?

HATCHET

Duly noted-you respect your wife
Yet told me you never loved her
That conversation changed my life
I was the battle you would conquer

You kept telling me you couldn't cheat
That you needed to fight for your family
Words like lyrics to a song put on repeat
What you were doing you couldn't see

Despite not being physical, it was emotional
I was another woman and a best-kept secret
Yet in the end, you deemed me as irrational
You just couldn't own *your* mangled mindset

Continue to cohabitate in confusion
Acting all picture perfect and proud
Pompous and embodied in delusion
All because you promised and vowed

Deciding to mark me as absent
Destroying what you deserved
All the wasted time I had spent
A dead marriage you preserved

Will you remember or regret?
You made a decision to forget
To my heart you took a hatchet
With precision and a sharp set

11/3/17

FUCK

Fuck these tumultuous thoughts
Fuck my stomach always in knots

Fuck my gratitude
Fuck your attitude

Fuck my stupid mistake
Fuck all this heartache

Fuck my paralysis
Fuck our analysis

Fuck my devotion
Fuck each emotion

Fuck my attention
Fuck your deflection

Fuck your stability
Fuck your inability

Fuck all my deficiencies
Fuck your inconsistencies

Fuck your remorse
Fuck your "divorce"

Fuck every intention
Fuck every mention

Fuck your deception
Fuck my misconception

Fuck your selection
Fuck my rejection

Fuck your respect
Fuck your neglect

Fuck how I was naive
Fuck what I believe

Fuck all that I feel
Fuck what was real

Fuck your pretending
Fuck whatever ending

11/4/17

OBJECT

They usually fall for me too quickly
They always tend to leave abruptly
When my roses' thorns get too prickly
Going on to crush my heart corruptly

They do as they wish and then dispose
Finishing me off with demonic defeat
Triumphantly battered from their blows
Conquering me through cowardly deceit

I am an *object* desired that they destroy
An *object* of lust they latch to and abuse
Ruined remnants and wreckage they enjoy
When they abandon me and let me loose

They make me hungry for them to devour
Flustering me with thoughts they provoke
Their consumption eventually grows sour
Disgusted by me, they *diminish* and revoke

I trek through the turbulence and instability
Filtered thoughts they deprive and stimulate
Leaving me discharged in harm and humility
Choosing to be ruthless to me and repudiate

AMUSEMENT

I just stepped off of your radical rollercoaster
After repeatedly riding it for too damn long
Didn't get souvenirs or an autographed poster
Only inconsistent mind fucks that gone wrong

Struggling for power and lacking trust
I had to step off of this nauseating ride
Blind turns made me sick from disgust
Twisting and spinning by a gutless guide

Here we go, up and down, round and round
Jerking me back and forth loosened my grip
Holding on tight, trying to stand my ground
Bruised and broken, everything begins to slip

I go on and watch from the crowd
Debating if I want to ride it again
You made it clear I'm not allowed
I head back to where I always begin

CONDUCTOR

The instrument you play is your word
Reading my notes, the pitch is *"naïve"*
Musical scale of a wounded songbird
A somber symphony of make-believe

A performance carefully orchestrated
Listening in awe and childlike fascination
Unaware I was subliminally desecrated
I was ***diminished*** with no standing ovation

Conducting a poised, melodic harmony
Soon your chorus would be ***catastrophic***
Stirring up sounds of my ***melancholy***
Changing the tune to evil and dystrophic

Now I produce as I pay you a tribute
You are *subject matter* I call demonic
A claim you would naturally refute
Take a seat, it's *Melissa's Harmonic*

WAR

Words, not actions were your weapon of choice
Shot a hole right through my fucking black heart
As you would march on in verbiage and a voice
Ripping and breaking every piece left of me apart

Your language was a noose choking me out
You walked away with not one single scar
I suffered from your brutal blows and bout
Blinded and bound to see who you really are

Communication that would cut me like a knife
Every insult flung was a ticking time bomb
Continuing to hurl grenades as I clung to life
You had so much wrath and too much napalm

Now my carnage decorates your destruction
Blown bits of me to fertilize your landscape
Why couldn't you just opt for an abduction
A prisoner of war who didn't get to escape

RESURRECTION

Six months later and now you're back
I suddenly suffer another heart attack

Why was I witnessing a resurrection?
Warmly giving me so much affection

Reliving all of the pain and heartache
We had an agreement that we'd break

You did not follow my one happy rule
Yet your love for me made me a fool

She lies with leukemia in a hospital bed
It's fucked up that you want me instead

You tell me she has no one in her life except for you
Yet how long will you keep lying and being untrue?

What about me? I don't have anyone here
I push you away and you come back near

Just because I am independent and strong
Does not mean it is okay to drag me along

Stay in your state of sexless dependency
Or step up and only have one tendency

DEPENDENCY

Brushed off one too many times
Not faring well with being ignored
You act as if I perpetrated crimes
Why was I the one you explored?

Why did I grow so dependent?
I see you've made me just like her
Yet she remains the one defendant
Whom you tend, nurture, and foster

I guess her and I are both pathetic and weak
Yet, I am stronger and can actually be alone
I am wild and she is the woman who is meek
Fuck you, I will just handle this on my own

UNKNOWN

When she says jump, you say, "how high?"
Staying with a leech who sucks out your soul
I continue to wait and time slowly ticks by
As you clearly define my "supporting role"

I hate a woman I do not even know
Her presence somewhat haunts me
I know I need to finally let you go
Yet they say that "three is company"

Is it you or her that continues to cling?
Which one of you is so damn needy?
I am the infatuation and just a fling
Engaging in behaviors somewhat seedy

What happened that forced you away?
Both of us are being blindly misled
Due to your obligation to her you stay
But you fuck me in my head and bed

Does she not have one fucking clue?
Does she have that thick of a skull?
What words of yours are even true?
I was just a conquest and a set goal

You two can obviously not be apart
Possessing zero ability to be alone
Playing the dutiful man from the start
Why can't you cope if you're alone?

You keep telling me that it's "done with"
I am still waiting for you stop cowering
Yet, your grand finale is another myth
Leaving me to see you're disempowering

I want her to get out of your life and gone
It's making me helpless, volatile, and insane
Yet you are the player and I am the pawn
Getting a good fuck by penetrating my brain

Look at all of the destruction you've caused
Each crisis causes you a senseless convulsion
Then I, your hidden agenda, again gets paused
Because of your tendency and your compulsion

I will be the dark damsel dancing in destruction
The one who is never the first to ever be chosen
My heart will always be the victim of abduction
Unable to love again because I've become frozen

WOUNDED BIRD

You once mentioned you were drawn to those afflicted
To what you labeled the symptoms of a "*wounded bird*"
As we grew closer, I could see us both were conflicted
The more frequent our whirlwind interaction occurred

It dawned on me that I was a bird with a wounded wing
You kept reiterating I was not ***damaged***, a healing ritual
Reassuring me that I had meaning, that I was something
As our communication grew and became more habitual

I was the bird who would peck and gawk
Every time you'd put pressure on the pain
So stubborn and bitchy, more like a hawk
You wouldn't give up in sun, snow, or rain

One day, you left the cage open and went away
I waited for my rescuer to return and to repair
Wondering what I had done wrong every day
You lost patience with my darkness and despair

Did you forget me because I was too broken?
Unforgiveable, you chose to not stick around
So many words I wanted to say went unspoken
When I tried to fly, I weakly fell to the ground

I was more hurt and felt such unbearable harm
My rescue you felt was not worth taking a risk
I wanted to land, but you pulled back your arm
Not wanting to save me, scoop me up to whisk

Facing the fact that you were never coming back
I decided I would be my one and only true savior
The shade of my wings may always be dark black
However, I'm now bolder, bigger, and much braver

NEED

You say you need me in your life
Well, I do not need you in mine
One major obstacle is your wife
I have my demons, but I am fine

My mind runs like a hamster in a wheel
Over, over, and over, round and round
I'm constantly wondering how you feel
The noise of silence is a blaring sound

I go fucking insane when you choose to ignore
My existence, you've brushed off and banished
What the fuck do you even play mind games for?
I question what I have done and why you vanished

You said you need me in your life
I don't need, but want you in mine
Then I start to think of all this strife
Now I know I must quickly resign

SECOND PLACE

I am the woman that is never chosen
Never winning the gold or first place
People ask me why I'm cold and frozen
It is because I lag behind in every race

Never one to ever be the first choice
They are drawn to my independence
Basking in my freedom, they rejoice
Not subservient I then lose attendance

My independence drives them away
I am never over, I am always under
All talk and no action, I never sway
Backpedaling from me, their blunder

I never get the glory or the gold
Silver is the only medal I wear
Now their stories are getting told
As they left me just standing there

DRAWN TO DARKNESS

Behind those dark set of eyes
I can see your darkness lies

I should have known better
I saw you in a scarlet letter

Like a magnet, every dark soul is drawn
To me, and we partake in a dreaded liaison

You made certain to stomp me when I was down
Guaranteeing my place in the darkness to drown

Not enough, you then spit in my fucking face
In two minutes, reiterating that I was a disgrace

Nailing my coffin of self-doubt securely shut
Watching me bleed from the words you'd cut

You left me for dead and struggling for air
I've risen and a poetic war I hereby declare